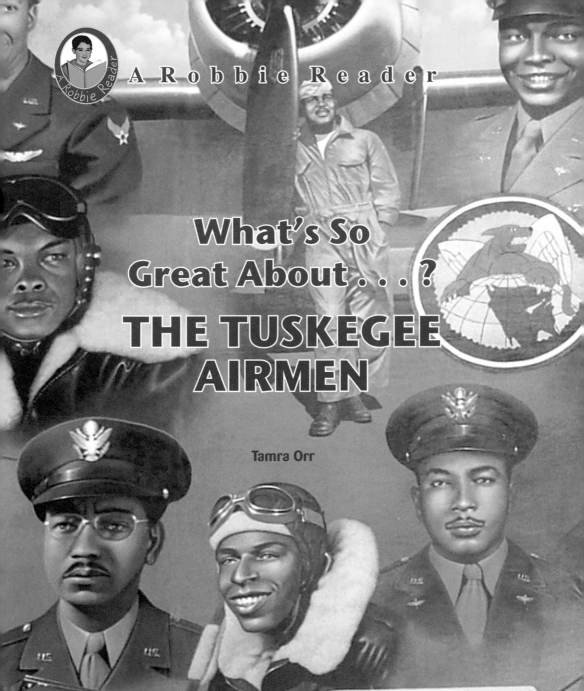

A Robbie Reader

What's So
Great About . . . ?
THE TUSKEGEE
AIRMEN

Tamra Orr

Mitchell Lane
PUBLISHERS
P.O. Box 196
Hockessin, Delaware 19707
Visit us on the web: www.mitchelllane.com
Comments? email us: mitchelllane@mitchelllane.com

PUBLISHERS

Printing   1   2   3   4   5   6   7   8   9

A Robbie Reader
What's So Great About . . . ?

Amelia Earhart	Anne Frank	Annie Oakley
Barack Obama	The Buffalo Soldiers	Christopher Columbus
Daniel Boone	Davy Crockett	The Donner Party
Elizabeth Blackwell	Ferdinand Magellan	Francis Scott Key
Galileo	George Washington Carver	Harriet Tubman
Helen Keller	Henry Hudson	Jacques Cartier
Johnny Appleseed	King Tut	Lewis and Clark
Martin Luther King Jr.	Michelle Obama	Paul Bunyan
Pocahontas	Robert Fulton	Rosa Parks
Sam Houston	**The Tuskegee Airmen**	

Library of Congress Cataloging-in-Publication Data
Orr, Tamra.
  What's so great about the Tuskegee Airmen / by Tamra Orr.
    p. cm. — (A Robbie reader) (What's so great about — ?)
  Includes bibliographical references and index.
  ISBN 978-1-58415-832-5 (library bound)
 1. World War, 1939-1945 — Participation, African American — Juvenile literature. 2. United States. Army Air Forces. Fighter Squadron, 99th — History — Juvenile literature. 3. African American air pilots — History — Juvenile literature. 4. World War, 1939-1945 — Aerial operations, American — Juvenile literature. 5. Tuskegee Army Air Field (Ala.) — Juvenile literature. 6. World War, 1939-1945 — Campaigns — Western Front — Juvenile literature. 7. World War, 1939-1945 — Regimental histories — United States — Juvenile literature. I. Title.
  D810.N4O75 2010
  940.54'4973 — dc22

2009027360

ABOUT THE AUTHOR: Tamra Orr has written nearly 200 nonfiction books for readers of all ages, including *What's So Great About the Buffalo Soldiers?* for Mitchell Lane Publishers. She graduated from Ball State University in Indiana with a degree in English and Secondary Education. Now she lives in the Pacific Northwest with her four kids, husband, dog, and cat.

PUBLISHER'S NOTE: The following story has been thoroughly researched and to the best of our knowledge represents a true story. Documentation of such research is on page 29. While every possible effort has been made to ensure accuracy, the publisher will not assume liability for damages caused by inaccuracies in the data, and makes no warranty on the accuracy of the information contained herein.

TABLE OF CONTENTS

Chapter One
A Special Passenger 5

Chapter Two
They Wanted to Fly 9

Chapter Three
The Tuskegee Experiment 13

Chapter Four
Meet the "Red Tails" 17

Chapter Five
Of Civil Rights and Presidents 23

Timeline in History 28
Find Out More 29
     Books 29
     Works Consulted 29
     On the Internet 30
Glossary 31
Index 32

Words in **bold** type can be found in the glossary.

A delighted Eleanor Roosevelt enjoys her ride through the sky with pilot Charles Alfred Anderson, who taught himself to fly at the age of twenty-two. He had become well known for his goodwill flights to Cuba, Jamaica, Haiti, and six other countries before joining Tuskegee University as Chief Flight Instructor.

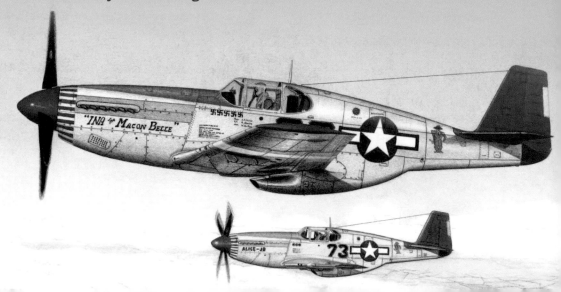

A Special Passenger

The President's Secret Service men were not happy. Eleanor Roosevelt, the President's wife, was being difficult.

It had not started out that way, of course. Mrs. Roosevelt had stopped by Alabama's Tuskegee (tuh-SKEE-gee) University for a quick visit. No one knew that she would change history while she was there.

It was March 29, 1941. The United States was already involved in what would one day be called World War II. The First Lady had stopped to meet the school's black students. She also wanted to ask them what was on many people's minds. Could black people really be pilots? There was no question the armed services needed all the pilots they could get in the coming battles. However, a number of people did not believe that blacks were smart enough or brave enough to fly airplanes.

Finally, Mrs. Roosevelt turned to Charles Alfred "Chief" Anderson, the head of Tuskegee University's **aviation** (ay-vee-AY-shun) program. Was it truly possible for blacks to fly? He replied, "Certainly we can!" To prove his point, he invited her to take a ride with him. She said yes. When she climbed in the back of his Piper Cub plane, her Secret Service men were not happy. They quickly called the President.

The Piper Cub plane dates to 1927 when two brothers wanted a lightweight plane for barnstorming. Years later, the company was purchased by William Piper. Soon the aircraft became the primary aircraft of the Civilian Pilot Training program.

Tuskegee University was the first black college to be named both a National Historic Landmark and a National Historic Site. Besides being famous for training airmen, the university is where George Washington Carver conducted his revolutionary peanut experiments.

"Well, if she wants to do it, there's nothing we can do to stop her," he said.

For the next 40 minutes, Mrs. Roosevelt flew with Anderson. When they landed, she was smiling. She had her picture taken with the chief. Then she went home to the White House. She wanted to talk to her husband.

Soon the decision to teach the first group of black men how to fly was announced. The hundreds of pilots who became the Tuskegee Airmen had a First Lady to thank. Her short flight led to victories in war—and jump-started the civil rights movement in the United States.

OER THE RAMPARTS WE WATCH

UNITED · STATES
ARMY AIR FORCES

This World War II poster for the U.S. Air Force attracted many young Americans who wanted to defend their country from above the clouds. That wish to fight was felt by many, no matter their race or gender.

They Wanted to Fly

As the 1930s ended, the people of the United States were worried. Times were hard. For ten years, people had struggled to stay alive. Thousands had lost their jobs, and families stood in line for food. Then it became clear that a war being fought in other countries was about to include the United States. Germany's leader, Adolf Hitler, was taking control of many European countries. The United States, along with **allies** France, Great Britain, and Russia, prepared to fight back.

Battles were fought on the ground and in the sky. Pilots who could fly swiftly, aim carefully, and escape completely were in high demand. All white men who wanted to be pilots were asked to join the armed services. In 1939, Congress passed the Civilian Pilot Training Act.

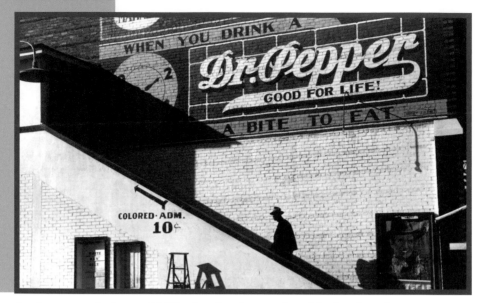

A photograph from 1939 clearly shows that blacks faced segregation every day in a number of ways. Even movie theaters had separate entrances for blacks and whites.

It provided funds to colleges across the country for training thousands of students to be military pilots. Blacks, however, were not invited.

During this period in history, blacks were still thought of as **inferior** to, or less important than, whites. They were not allowed to sit with whites on buses or use the same areas as whites. Some people believed that blacks simply were not smart enough to learn how to do something as technical as flying a plane.

These people were wrong. Many black men were eager to help win the war by taking to the skies. They wanted to learn. They wanted to be called on to help their country. After Eleanor Roosevelt's visit to Tuskegee University, they were finally given that chance.

Alabama's Tuskegee University was founded in 1881 by Booker T. Washington, a man who had been a slave. After the Civil War, Washington spent much of his time teaching others the importance of freedom. At Tuskegee, he taught black men and women to reach for their dreams—including those of flying through the clouds in airplanes.

Booker T. Washington was a role model for many of the country's blacks. He helped change the education system throughout the United States.

Howard A. Wooten dons the pilot's distinctive cap and goggles for his graduation photograph from the U.S. Army Negro Air Corps training school at Tuskegee.

The Tuskegee Experiment

In 1939, all-black colleges were given money to pay for pilot training programs. One of the first was Tuskegee University. It used the funds to build a new base. It had an airfield, mess halls where students ate, and **barracks** where they slept. It also had a hospital, grocery store, and theater.

Not everyone liked these programs. Some fully expected the students to fail. They called the program "The Tuskegee Experiment."

Tuskegee's students were trained by Charles Alfred Anderson. In 1933, he had been one of the first pilots to fly round-trip from Atlantic City, New Jersey, to Los Angeles, California. The first class began training in August 1941.

Students found out how weather worked. They were taught how to **navigate**. They studied science, **engineering**, and maps. They practiced taking off and landing. Most importantly, they were shown how to strafe. Strafing involved flying very low, quickly firing a lot of rounds at targets on the ground and in the air. When the students graduated after nine months of training, they made up the 99th Fighter **Squadron**.

99th
Fighter Squadron Patch

On December 7, 1941, the Japanese bombed Pearl Harbor, a naval base in Hawaii. Many Americans were killed in this attack. A few days later, the United States officially entered World War II. The Tuskegee Airmen waited to be called to action. It took a long time.

Of the thirteen original cadets, five graduated in 1942 (from left): Capt. Benjamin O. Davis Jr., 2nd Lt. Lemuel R. Custis, 2nd Lt. George S. Roberts, 2nd Lt. Charles H. DeBow, and 2nd Lt. Mac Ross. Davis, whose father was the first African American general of the U.S. Army, would become the first African American general of the U.S. Air Force.

In April 1943, the 99th finally began receiving orders for the many missions they would fly. They went to North Africa to strafe targets. They were sent to Italy to help protect troops on the ground. Although they did their jobs perfectly, some squadrons objected to flying with black pilots. They complained to the army. Finally the Chief of Staff ordered a review of how the 99th had performed. He found that the fighters of the 99th had done as well as— and often far better than—any other team. The Tuskegee Experiment was a real success.

Tuskegee Airmen go over their orders at Ramitelli, Italy, in March 1945. Pictured in the front row are Jimmie D. Wheeler (with goggles) and Emile G. Clifton (cloth cap). Standing left to right are Ronald W. Reeves (cloth cap); Hiram Mann (leather cap); Joseph L. "Joe" Chineworth (wheel cap); Elwood T. Driver (speaking); Edward "Ed" Thomas (partial view); and Woodrow W. Crockett (wheel cap).

Meet the "Red Tails"

Every day, the Tuskegee Airmen flew missions that saved lives and protected troops from the enemy. The 99th Fighter Squadron was combined with the 100th, 301st, and 302nd squadrons. This created the all-black 332nd Fighter Group. Together, these men developed one of the best records in army history.

Despite their record, when black pilots returned to land, they still had to face **segregation** (seh-greh-GAY-shun). They were not allowed to train or fight alongside the white military men. They often encountered **prejudice** (PREH-joo-dis) when on the ground.

The men of the 332nd painted the tails of their aircraft red to let others know who they were. Soon, they were known as the Red Tails.

In January 1944, the Red Tails took part in a battle in Italy. Over several days, they destroyed eight German planes and shot down even more. They performed perfectly—and word began to spread about these pilots.

Stories of the black airmen appeared in newspapers and on radio programs around the United States. Slowly, Tuskegee Airmen gained the honor and respect they deserved. It was not long before white bomber pilots were

Tuskegee Airman Red Tail P-51 Mustang

especially asking for the Red Tails to fly with them. Soon their nickname changed to the Red Tail Angels.

By the time World War II ended, almost 1,000 black pilots had graduated from Tuskegee University. Hundreds of others had been trained to be radio repairmen, engine mechanics, parachute riggers, control tower operators, and other important aviation personnel. These brave men flew in more than

Captains Lemuel R. Custis (left) and Charles B. Hall were both members of the 99th Fighter Squadron. In one year starting June 4, 1943, their squadron flew more than 3,000 missions, damaging six planes and shooting down 17 more.

During a briefing at an Italian base, an officer points out German targets for the pilots in the 15th U.S. Army Air Force.

15,000 battle flights and 1,500 missions. They destroyed more than one hundred German planes in the air and even more on the ground. They had an excellent record, losing only 66 lives in combat. The Red Tails earned many medals, including more than one hundred Distinguished Flying Crosses, fourteen Bronze Stars, and eight Purple Hearts.

When the war was over and the pilots were back on the ground, they still had to cope with a country that felt blacks were inferior. This was hard to face, but that attitude was about to start changing.

EXECUTIVE ORDER

ESTABLISHING THE PRESIDENT'S COMMITTEE ON
EQUALITY OF TREATMENT AND OPPORTUNITY IN
THE ARMED SERVICES

WHEREAS it is essential that there be maintained in the armed services of the United States the highest standards of democracy, with equality of treatment and opportunity for all those who serve in our country's defense:

NOW, THEREFORE, by virtue of the authority vested in me as President of the United States, by the Constitution and the statutes of the United States, and as Commander in Chief of the armed services, it is hereby ordered as follows:

1. It is hereby declared to be the policy of the President that there shall be equality of treatment and opportunity for all persons in the armed services without regard to race, color, religion or national origin. This policy shall be put into effect as rapidly as possible, having due regard to the time required to effectuate any necessary changes without impairing efficiency or morale.

2. There shall be created in the National Military Establishment an advisory committee to be known as the President's Committee on Equality of Treatment and Opportunity in the Armed Services, which shall be composed of seven members to be designated by the President.

3. The Committee is authorized on behalf of the President to examine into the rules, procedures and practices of the armed services in order to determine in what respect such rules, procedures and practices may be altered or improved with a view to carrying out the policy of this order. The Committee shall confer and advise with the Secretary of Defense, the Secretary

The purpose of Truman's Executive Order 9981 echoed in newspaper headlines as the President started the official process of ending segregation in the military. By late 1954, there were no more all-black units.

Of Civil Rights and Presidents

Once the war was over, President Harry S. Truman made a big decision. On July 26, 1948, he signed **Executive** (ek-ZEK-yoo-tiv) **Order** 9981. It stated that all people in the armed services should receive equal treatment and opportunity. He commanded that all soldiers were to be treated equally, regardless of their race, color, religion or **national origin**. No longer were they to be trained and housed separately. Thanks to the hard work of the Tuskegee Airmen, segregation, or separation of the races, was coming to an end.

Executive Order 9981 was one of the most important steps in the civil rights movement. With many people in the nation fighting to

In 2007, at the U.S. Capitol, President George W. Bush presented the Congressional Gold Medal to Dr. Roscoe Brown Jr., former commander of the 100th Squadron of the 332nd Fighter Group. He accepted the medal on behalf of all the Tuskegee Airmen.

make sure every person was given the same rights and treated equally, the change in the military set an example. It rippled through the country like a stone thrown into a pond. Other important steps followed, including the **desegregation** (dee-seh-greh-GAY-shun) of America's schools.

By 2009, more than 60 years after the first class of airmen arrived at Tuskegee, there were only 330 pilots and ground crew left. They were in their eighties and nineties. In

2007, their contribution to U.S. history was noted in a speech by then Illinois Senator Barack Obama. He said, "My career in public service was made possible by the path heroes like the Tuskegee Airmen trail-blazed."

Two years later, when Obama was sworn in as the nation's 44th president, he remembered the Tuskegee Airmen. He requested that they be invited to his **inauguration** (in-aw-gyur-AY-shun) ceremony.

After watching President Barack Obama take his oath of office in Washington on January 20, 2009, members of the Tuskegee Airmen sang the national anthem.

"They served honorably on behalf of our country, helped fight the battle to overcome racial **barriers** and because of the historic nature of this election, they deserve to be there," stated a White House official.

The invitation was an honor that meant a great deal to these men. They had willingly offered their lives, skills, and bravery to protect a country that had not yet given them equal rights. The Tuskegee Airmen's efforts and determination helped further the goals of the civil rights movement—and the rights of human beings throughout the nation.

Clockwise, from left: P-39 Airacobra, 1942–1944; P-47 Thunderbolt, 1944; P-40 Warhawk, 1942–1944; P-51 Mustang, 1944–1945

TIMELINE IN HISTORY

1881	Tuskegee University is founded by Booker T. Washington.
1932	Franklin D. Roosevelt is elected president of the United States. He will serve until 1945.
1933	Charles A. Anderson completes a round-trip flight between New Jersey and California.
1939	Britain and France declare war on Germany; the Civilian Pilot Training Act is passed by Congress.
1941	
March 29	Eleanor Roosevelt visits Tuskegee University, and Charles Anderson takes her on a ride in his Piper Cub.
July	The first pilot class arrives at Tuskegee University. Instruction begins on August 25.
December	The Japanese bomb Pearl Harbor; the U.S. enters World War II.
1942	
March	The first pilot class graduates from Tuskegee University.
1943	
April	The 99th Fighter Squadron receives its first battle orders.
1944	In January, the Red Tails begin gaining respect across the country.
1945	World War II ends on August 14.
1946	The last class of Tuskegee Airmen graduates on June 26.
1948	President Harry S. Truman signs Executive Order 9981.
1954	The armed forces are fully integrated.
2007	George W. Bush presents the Congressional Gold Medal to the surviving Tuskegee Airmen.
2009	The Tuskegee Airmen are invited as special guests to President Barack Obama's inauguration.

FIND OUT MORE

Books

De Capua, Sarah. *The Tuskegee Airmen: African American Pilots of World War II.* Mankato, Minnesota: Child's World, 2009.

Fleischman, John. *Black and White Airmen: Their True History.* New York: Houghton Mifflin Books for Children, 2007.

Hasday, Judy. *The Tuskegee Airmen.* New York: Chelsea House Publications, 2003.

Homan, Lynn. *Tuskegee Airmen: American Heroes.* Gretna, Louisiana: Pelican Publishing Company, 2002.

Johnson, Angela. *Wind Flyers.* New York: Simon and Schuster, 2007.

Works Consulted

Bucholtz, Chris. *332nd Fighter Group: Tuskegee Airmen.* Osprey Publishing, 2007.

Franklin D. Roosevelt Presidential Library and Museum: The Tuskegee Airmen
http://docs.fdrlibrary.marist.edu/tuskegee.html

Homan, Lynn. *Black Knights: The Story of the Tuskegee Airmen.* Gretna, Louisiana: Pelican Publishing, 2001.

Record, Kristen. "Southern Museum of Flight's Tuskegee Airmen Exhibit." NBC13.com, February 25, 2009.
http://www.nbc13.com/vtm/news/spirit_of_alabama/article/southern_museum_of_flights_tuskegee_airmen_exhibit/61123/

Seelye, Katharine. "Inauguration Is a Culmination for Black Airmen." December 9, 2008. *The New York Times.* http://www.nytimes.com/2008/12/10/us/politics/10inaug.html

"The Tuskegee Airmen 332nd Fighter Group"
www.acepilots.com/usaaf_tusk.html

Tuskegee Airmen, Inc.: The National Website of the Tuskegee Airmen
http://www.tuskegeeairmen.org/

U.S. Park Service: Tuskegee Airmen National Historic Site
http://www.nps.gov/tuai/

FIND OUT MORE

On the Internet

Legends of the Tuskegee Airmen
http://www.nps.gov/history/museum/exhibits/tuskegee/airoverview.htm

National Museum of the U.S. Air Force: Tuskegee Airmen Fact Sheet
http://www.nationalmuseum.af.mil/factsheets/factsheet.asp?id=1356

The Red Tail Project
www.redtail.org/airmen.html

Tuskegee Airmen Facts from Tuskegee University
http://www.tuskegee.edu/Global/story.asp?S=1127695

GLOSSARY

allies (AL-eyes)—People or groups who band together for a common cause. The 26 nations that fought against Germany and its allies in World War II were called the Allies, with a capital *A*.

aviation (ay-vee-AY-shun)—The design, development, production, operation, and use of aircraft.

barnstorm—To travel around the country giving shows or sight-seeing tours to passengers.

barracks (BAYR-aks)—A building or buildings used for lodging soldiers.

barriers (BAA-ree-urs)—Things that get in the way.

desegregation (dee-seh-greh-GAY-shun)—The outlawing of customs or practices in which different groups or races are kept separate.

engineering (en-jih-NEER-ing)—The use of technology and math to design or build machines, buildings, or other structures.

executive (ek-ZEK-yoo-tiv) **order**—A decision handed down by the president.

inauguration (in-aw-gyur-AY-shun)—The formal process of taking office, especially the office of United States president.

inferior (in-FEE-ree-ur)—Less than; less valuable or less important.

navigate (NAA-vih-gayt)—To direct or steer a ship, aircraft, or other vehicle in a desired direction.

national origin (NAA-shu-nul OR-ih-jin)—The country in which a person is born.

prejudice (PREH-joo-dis)—A negative feeling or opinion about someone based on his or her race, gender, or religion.

segregation (seh-greh-GAY-shun)—The practice of keeping people separate based on race, religion, or some other trait.

squadron (SKWAH-drun)—A unit of the U.S. Air Force, usually with two or more troops, a headquarters, and supporting units.

INDEX

99th Fighter Squadron   14, 15, 17, 20
100th Squadron   17, 24
301st Squadron   17
302nd Squadron   17
332nd Fighter Group   17, 24
Airacobra   26
Anderson, Charles Alfred   4, 6, 7, 13
Bronze Stars   21
Brown, Dr. Roscoe, Jr.   24
Bush, George W.   24
Chineworth, Joseph L. "Joe"   16
Civilian Pilot Training   6, 9
Civil rights movement   7, 23, 26
Civil War   11
Clifton, Emile G.   16
Congressional Gold Medal   24
Crockett, Woodrow W.   16
Custis, Lemuel R.   15, 20
Davis, Benjamin O., Jr.   15
Davis, Benjamin O., Sr.   15
DeBow, Charles H.   15
Desegregation   23, 24
Distinguished Flying Crosses   21
Driver, Elwood T.   16
Executive Order 9981   22, 23
Flying Crosses   21
France   9
Germany   9, 18

Great Britain   9
Hall, Charles B.   20
Hitler, Adolf   9
Italy   15, 16, 18, 21
Mann, Hiram   16
Mustang   18–19, 26
North Africa   15
Obama, Barack   25
Pearl Harbor   14
Piper Cub   6
Purple Hearts   21
Red Tail Angels   19, 21
Red Tails   17, 18–19
Reeves, Ronald W.   16
Roberts, George S.   15
Roosevelt, Eleanor   4, 5, 7, 11
Roosevelt, Franklin D.   5, 6–7
Ross, Mac   15
Russia   9
Segregation   10, 17, 22, 23, 24
Thomas, Edward "Ed"   16
Thunderbolt   26
Truman, Harry S.   22, 23
Tuskegee University   4, 5, 6, 7, 12, 13–15, 19, 24
Warhawk   26
Washington, Booker T.   11
Wheeler, Jimmie   16
Wooten, Howard A.   12
World War II   5, 8, 12, 14–15, 16, 17–19, 20, 21